PETER AND THE WOLF

Illustrated by Victor G Ambrus
Retold by James Riordan

Oxford University Press
Oxford Toronto Melbourne

Oxford University Press, Walton Street, Oxford OX2 6DP

Oxford New York Toronto
Petaling Jaya Singapore Hong Kong Tokyo
Delhi Bombay Calcutta Madras Karachi
Nairobi Dar es Salaam Cape Town
Melbourne Auckland

and associated companies in
Berlin Ibadan

Oxford is a trade mark of Oxford University Press

Illustrations © Victor G Ambrus 1986
Text © James Riordan 1986
First published 1986
First published in paperback 1989

British Library Cataloguing in Publication Data
Riordan, James
  Peter and the wolf.
  I. Title II. Ambrus, Victor III. Prokofiev,
  S.S. Peter and the wolf
  823'.914[J] PZ7
ISBN 0-19-279824-3 (Hardback)
ISBN 0-19-272201-8 (Paperback)

Typeset by Oxford Publishing Services
Printed in Hong Kong

PROLOGUE

There was once a Russian composer, Sergei Prokofiev. He wanted to write a piece of music to introduce children to the instruments of the orchestra. He thought the best way of doing this was to write a story and set music to it. The story is about a brave young boy named Peter, his Grandfather, three animal friends – a little bird, a duck and a cat – a band of huntsmen and a wicked wolf.

And as the composer himself explained:

'Each character in this fairy tale is represented by an instrument of the orchestra:

the bird by a *flute*,

the duck by an *oboe*,

the cat by a *clarinet*,

Grandfather by a *bassoon*,

the wolf by three *horns*,

Peter by the *violins*,

the huntsmen by the *drums*.'

So besides reading the story of Peter and the Wolf, see if you can match the words to music.

THE FAIRY TALE

Early one morning Peter opened the garden gate and went out into a big green meadow. Soon he saw his little friend the bird sitting in a nearby tree.

'How peaceful it is,' chirped the bird gaily.

Just then a duck came waddling up. Since Peter had left the gate open, she had come out too, fancying a swim in the deep meadow pond. On seeing the duck, the little bird flew down to the grass and landed beside her. He shrugged his shoulders and piped, 'What kind of bird are you if you cannot fly?'

To which the duck replied, 'And what kind of bird are you if you cannot swim?'

They dickered and bickered, the duck swimming round the pond, the bird hopping along the bank.

All of a sudden, something caught Peter's eye: it was a cat creeping through the grass. The cat was thinking to herself, 'While the bird is busy arguing, I'll creep up and catch him.'

So stealthily she crept closer and closer on her velvet paws. . .

'Look out!' shouted Peter.

In a trice the bird flew swiftly into the tree, while the duck quacked angrily at the cat from the middle of the pond.

The cat walked round and round the tree, musing to herself, 'Is it worth climbing up so high? By the time I get there, the bird will have flown away.'

Just then Grandfather came through the gate. He shouted angrily at Peter, 'Hey, don't you know this place is dangerous? What would you do if a wolf came out of the woods, eh?'

Peter took no notice: lads like him aren't scared of wolves. But Grandad grabbed his arm, bolted the gate fast behind him, and pulled him home.

No sooner had Peter gone than a big bad wolf *did* appear from out of the woods.

In a flurry of fur the cat scrambled up the tree.

But the poor duck ran squawking in her panic from the pond, helter-skelter. No matter how hard she ran she could not escape the wolf. He was coming closer and closer and closer . . . catching up with her . . . now pouncing and then – snap! – he caught her. And swallowed her in a single gulp.

Picture the scene now.

There was the cat sitting on one branch, the little bird on another – not too close to the cat – while the wolf stalked round and round the tree, glaring at them both with hungry eyes.

In the meantime, who should be watching but Peter, hiding behind the gate. He was not the least bit afraid. He ran home, fetched a big thick rope, and climbed on to the high stone wall. Now a branch of the tree round which the wolf was walking reached right to the wall. Taking hold of the branch, Peter nimbly swung himself into the tree.

'Dive down and fly round the wolf's nose,' said Peter to the bird. 'Only watch out he doesn't catch you.'

Almost brushing the wolf's nose with his wings, the bird flapped and fluttered just out of reach, while the wolf snapped furiously at him from this side and that. How that bird tormented the wolf, and how that wolf tried to catch him. But it was no use, the bird was too clever for him.

Meanwhile, Peter had made a loop at one end of the rope. He let it down carefully, caught the wolf by the tail and pulled. . .

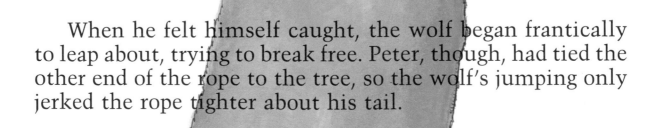

When he felt himself caught, the wolf began frantically to leap about, trying to break free. Peter, though, had tied the other end of the rope to the tree, so the wolf's jumping only jerked the rope tighter about his tail.

Right at that moment a band of huntsmen appeared from the trees. They had been on the wolf's trail and now, seeing him in the distance, they fired their guns: BANG, BANG, BANG!

'Stop shooting!' called Peter from the tree. 'Little bird and I have already caught the wolf. Just give us a hand to take him to the zoo.'

Picture now the triumphant procession. At the head came Peter, proud and bold. Then the huntsmen with the wolf. Last of all came Grandfather and the cat.

Old Grandad kept shaking his head, and grumbling, 'And if he hadn't caught the wolf, what then, eh?'

Above them all flew the little bird, chirping merrily, 'My, my, what brave fellows we are, Peter and I. See what we've caught!'

Hark . . . If you listen closely, you might just hear the duck quacking inside the wolf. For in his haste he had swallowed her alive and whole!

EPILOGUE

Prokofiev ended the story there. But what do you think happened next?

Before he went to Moscow Zoo, perhaps the wolf had an operation to free the poor duck, who came out safe and sound. Perhaps the wolf was stitched up and left to sulk in the Zoo Wolf Pen. Or maybe he escaped and lived out his days in deepest Siberia, far away from fearless boys like Peter.

Or what do you think? Perhaps you can make up a musical story about it yourself.